Cosmetic Surgery

Andrew Campbell

W

FRANKLIN WATTS
LONDON•SYDNEY

First published in 2008 by Franklin Watts

Franklin Watts
338 Euston Road
London NW1 3BH

Franklin Watts Australia
Level 17/207 Kent Street
Sydney NSW 2000

Dewey number: 617.9'5

ISBN: 978 0 7496 8270 5

Printed in China

A CIP catalogue record for this book
is available from the British Library

Franklin Watts is a division of Hachette Children's Books,
an Hachette Livre UK company.

www.hachettelivre.co.uk

Design: Billin Design Solutions
Editor in Chief: John C. Miles
Editor: Sarah Ridley
Art Director: Jonathan Hair
Picture research: Diana Morris

Picture credits:
Riccardo Azoury/Corbis: 36, 42-43. Bettmann/Corbis: 12. © British Association of
Aesthetic Plastic Surgeons: 31b. Burger/Phanie/Rex Features: 39. CC Studio/SPL: front
cover, 1, 18, 44. Creative/Getty Images: 35b. Foch/Phanie/Rex Features: 16.
Garo/Phanie/Rex Features: 23. Gillies Archives: 13. Dezo Hoffman/Rex Features: 25t.
Image Source/Rex Features: 19, 37, 38. Isopress/Senepart/Rex Features: 11. JSS
Images/BEI/Rex Features: 40. Martti Kainulainen/Rex Features: 2-3. James Lauritz/Getty
Images: 26. Wille Maldonado/Getty Images: 33cl, 33cr. Linda Matlow/Rex Features: 28.
Klaus Mellenthin/Rex Features: 27. Milk Photographie/Corbis: 17. Eric C Pendzich/Rex
Features: 41. Phanie/Rex Features: 29. Rex Features: 9, 20, 25b, 34. Gary Roberts/Rex
Features: 21. Alex Segre/Rex Features: 32. Ariel Skelly/Getty Images: 35tl. Sipa Press/Rex
Features: 14, 22, 24, 31t. Markku Ulander /Rex Features: 15. Universal/Everitt/Rex
Features: 10. Richard Young/Rex Features: 8. Markus Zeffler/Rex Features: 30.

CONTENTS

INTRODUCTION   8

ANCIENT ORIGINS   10

THE FIRST AND SECOND WORLD WARS   12

FROM HOLLYWOOD TO THE HIGH STREET   14

SURGICAL TREATMENTS   16

NON-SURGICAL TREATMENTS   18

THE BENEFITS   20

THE RISKS   22

SURGERY ADDICTS   24

TEENAGE SURGERY   26

CHECKS AND BALANCES   28

THE SURGEONS   30

VIEWING FIGURES   32

"THE BEAUTY MYTH"   34

BOOM AND BUST   36

ALTERNATIVES   38

FACING THE FUTURE   40

GLOSSARY   42

WEBSITES   43

INDEX   44

BOOB JOBS AND BOTOX,

tummy tucks and facelifts... The familiarity of these phrases tells us how much cosmetic surgery has become an everyday part of our lives. We read about celebrities' changing appearances in gossip magazines, watch ordinary men and women undergo extreme transformations on TV makeover shows, and even read horror stories in newspapers and on websites about cosmetic surgery procedures that go wrong.

GET SOME DEFINITION

But what exactly is cosmetic surgery? Basically, it is an operation or operations to modify an aspect of someone's appearance, for example to smooth out wrinkles on the face or remove unwanted areas of fat on the body. A broader definition includes non-surgical treatments that do not require a surgeon or doctor to perform them. Importantly – and unlike plastic surgery (see box) – such procedures are usually not medically necessary: they are a matter of personal choice.

▲ Media celebrities, such as Jordan, regularly hit the headlines for their cosmetic surgery treatments.

LET'S FACE IT

One of the biggest arguments in favour of cosmetic surgery is that operations and treatments help people to feel more confident about themselves. Millions of people agree with this; Americans spend between $12 billion and $15 billion each year on cosmetic surgery and non-surgical treatments. A survey in the UK in 2005 found that nearly half of all women and one-quarter of men would consider cosmetic surgery.

PRICE TO PAY

None of this is risk-free, however. Cosmetic surgery, like any other form of surgery, can go wrong. US hip-hop star Kanye West's mother, Donda, died in 2007 after cosmetic surgery that she may not have been healthy enough to receive. There are also psychological risks associated with cosmetic surgery and non-surgical treatments, with people having operations that they don't need and may regret.

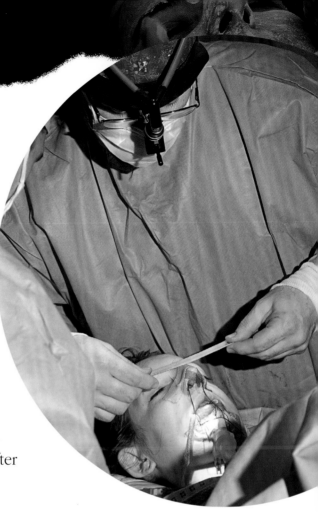

▲ Cosmetic surgery is largely safe, but all surgery carries risks.

COSMETIC vs PLASTIC SURGERY

Cosmetic surgery shares the same origins as plastic surgery, and techniques developed by cosmetic surgeons can be of great use to plastic surgeons. But there are big differences between the two. For one thing, plastic surgeons are concerned with reconstructing people's faces and bodies after accidents (for example, explosions) or illnesses (for example, cancers) that can cause severe scarring. Plastic surgeons also work with people born with disfigurements. The other big difference is training. All plastic surgeons are trained in general and specialist plastic surgery. The same is true for the best cosmetic surgeons – especially those who belong to professional associations – but in many countries, doctors with little or no surgical skills can practise as cosmetic surgeons.

MEN AND WOMEN have always tried to improve on what nature has given them, cutting and stretching parts of the body and using powders, creams and dyes to colour the skin. The reasons for doing this are as ancient as humanity: for worship and ritual, for belonging to the group and to fit in with ideals of beauty.

ANCIENT HINDUS

The origins of plastic and cosmetic surgery date back to ancient India. A traditional Hindu punishment for adultery was amputation of the nose, so surgeons developed a technique of cutting a replacement piece of skin from the victim's forehead or cheek and stitching it onto the stump where the nose had been.

TOXIC TUDORS

Queen Elizabeth I of England (1533–1603) was responsible for popularising an extreme form of make-up with deadly effects. This was the fashion for women to use a cream to make their faces pale white. The cream contained egg white, vinegar and powdered white lead, which caused scars and in some cases even death from lead poisoning.

◀ Queen Elizabeth I of England, as portrayed by actress Cate Blanchett. Elizabeth wore poisonous make-up to whiten her face.

GET THE FACTS STRAIGHT

- c.600 BCE: The Indian surgeon Sushruta describes using skin grafts from the cheek to reconstruct the nose.

- 4th century CE: The Greek physician Oribasius writes a medical encyclopaedia which includes different procedures for facial reconstruction.

- 16th century: The Italian surgeon Gasparo Tagliacozzi re-develops the ancient Indian procedure for nasal reconstruction.

- 1840s: General anaesthetics used for the first time in surgery. They produce a loss of feeling and reduce the pain of surgery, broadening the scope of operations.

- 1914–18: Plastic surgery techniques are developed to deal with the huge range of injuries surgeons encounter during the First World War.

TRADITION TODAY

In some cultures people have been adapting their bodies in the same way for centuries. The Padaung women of Myanmar (formerly Burma), for example, wear brass neck rings that stretch their necks to a length of up to 40 cm. Padaung women do this for religious reasons: long necks symbolise their ancestry to a snake-like dragon, believed to be the founder of the Padaung people.

▶ A Padaung woman from Myanmar wearing brass neck rings.

THE FIRST AND SECOND WORLD WARS

IT IS A SOBERING THOUGHT that many of the techniques used by today's plastic and cosmetic surgeons were pioneered during the two world wars by doctors working with mutilated soldiers.

▲ A First World War field hospital. Many plastic and cosmetic surgery techniques were developed in response to horrific war injuries.

FIRST WORLD WAR (1914–18)

Imagine the scene. A young soldier kneels in a waterlogged trench, then a mortar bomb explodes metres away from him. His steel helmet saves his life, but his face is ripped open by the blast. The widespread use in the First World War of grenades, mortar bombs and, above all, machine guns, led to injuries that most surgeons had never encountered before. Young soldiers in their thousands lost eyes, teeth, jaws and cheeks, as well as arms and legs. Doctors needed to find new ways to help them back to health.

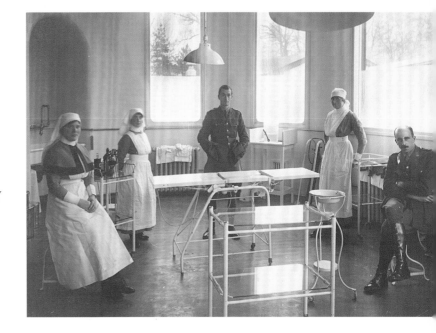

► Sir Harold Gillies (far right) in the operating theatre where he did most of his pioneering work.

SIR HAROLD GILLIES

One of the pioneers of plastic surgery during the First World War was the New Zealander Sir Harold Gillies. Gillies led a team of surgeons, based in Kent in south-east England, who developed a procedure called the pedicle skin graft. In this technique, skin and body tissue remain attached to the site from which they are taken to keep them nourished with blood until the new graft at the site of the injury "takes". Gillies also worked with artists and sculptors to make prosthetic (artificial) faces for soldiers with badly damaged features.

SECOND WORLD WAR (1939–45)

The Second World War gave rise to similarly horrific wounds and disfigurements. New explosives and fighter aircraft technology meant that surgeons faced fresh challenges dealing with wounded soldiers and pilots, particularly with severe burns that required extensive skin grafts. Gillies' cousin, Archibald McIndoe, was one of the Second World War's most notable plastic surgeons. He developed new techniques but also focused on the care and rehabilitation of his patients after surgery.

FACING THE ISSUES

Plastic surgery was vital for many people in the Second World War. Nowhere was this more the case than for the survivors of the atomic bomb attacks on the Japanese cities of Hiroshima and Nagasaki, in August 1945. Ten years after the attacks, 25 disfigured women from Hiroshima, dubbed the "Hiroshima Maidens" by the newspapers, travelled to the Mount Sinai Hospital in New York for plastic surgery. Surgeons performed about 140 operations to rebuild the women's noses, eyelids, lips, hands and other body parts. One of the women, Shigeko Sasamori, speaking in 1999, said, "... one third of my body was burned, especially my neck and hands." After surgery, she added, "I was able to marry and give birth to a son."

FROM HOLLYWOOD TO THE HIGH STREET

BY THE END of the Second World War, thanks in part to the growing demands of the entertainment industry, it was a short step from plastic surgery to cosmetic surgery. Techniques for treating disfigurement were adopted to make men and women more symmetrical, more youthful and more glamorous.

MADE FOR THE MOVIES

One of the first Hollywood stars known to have cosmetic surgery to improve his appearance for the camera was the actor and singer Dean Martin, who in 1948 made his film debut after a nose job operation. Other 1930s and 1940s movie stars rumoured to have had face-lifts included Joan Crawford and Marlene Dietrich. In the early 1960s Marilyn Monroe had a chin implant. By now cosmetic surgery was on its way to becoming a standard procedure for Hollywood actors and actresses.

▲ Actress Marilyn Monroe, whose chin implant in the early 1960s was part of the first wave of celebrity cosmetic surgery.

GROWING APPEAL

In the 1970s and 1980s, more and more ordinary people began to have cosmetic surgery. Today, cosmetic surgery has gone from being a guilty secret to which few people admit, to an everyday part of life. Some groups of people have more cosmetic surgery than others, however. According to a survey in the USA in 2006, 90% of cosmetic surgery patients were women, while just over half were aged 51 or older. The survey also found that 77% of people having cosmetic procedures were white.

CHANGING ATTITUDES

Until recently, celebrities – like everyone else – have been reluctant to admit having cosmetic surgery or non-surgical treatments, but that may be changing. In 2007, "X-Factor" judge Simon Cowell admitted having Botox injections, while actress Scarlett Johansson said she would definitely have cosmetic surgery when she was older because, as she said, "I don't want to look like an old hag."

WHAT DO YOU THINK?

- What reasons can you think of for the growing popularity of cosmetic surgery?

- What famous people can you think of who have had cosmetic surgery? Do you know if they have had this for a fact, or is this just media rumour?

- Why do you think people may be embarrassed about admitting to having cosmetic surgery? Would you be?

▼ Young or old, fat or thin, cosmetic surgery is now available to all who can afford it.

THERE ARE A LARGE number of procedures that cosmetic surgeons can carry out. They range from the well-known, such as breast implants, to the less familiar, such as umbilicoplasty (to correct a sticking-out belly button).

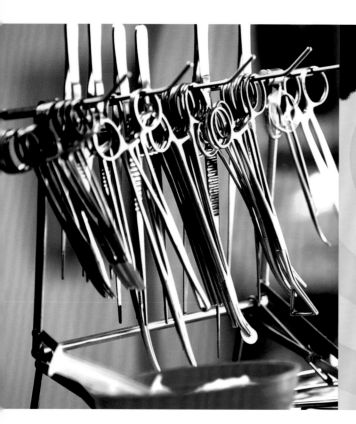

GET THE FACTS STRAIGHT

The top five cosmetic surgery procedures in the USA in 2006 were:

- Liposuction (403,684 operations),
- Breast enlargement (383,886 operations),
- Eyelid surgery (209,999 operations),
- Tummy tuck (172,457 operations),
- Breast reduction (145,822 operations).

(Source: The American Society for Aesthetic Plastic Surgery)

FACE-LIFTS AND MORE

Cosmetic surgery operations on the face include face-, neck- and brow-lifts, nose jobs, pinning back or altering ears, and eye surgery to get rid of hooded eyelids or large eye bags. People usually opt for face-lifts to reduce flabby skin and smooth out the jaw line. The operation can last up to six hours. The surgeon makes an incision (cut) in the skin from the patient's hairline to behind the ears, before pulling the skin up and back into its new position. The surgeon then closes the incision with fine stitches.

BODY OPS

Surgical procedures for the body include breast enlargement and reduction, buttock lifts and genital reshaping. Breasts are usually enlarged by using implants filled with artificial liquids or gels. In 2006 the USA lifted its 14-year ban on silicone breast implants. It had imposed the ban after complaints that the implants leaked and made some women ill.

FAT CHANCE

Cosmetic surgery operations to remove fat are extremely popular in Western countries, where obesity is a major problem. In the USA, for example, liposuction is the most popular cosmetic surgery procedure. Liposuction involves a surgeon inserting a small tube called a cannula into the skin, in areas such as the neck, upper arms, thighs or abdomen. The cannula breaks up the fat cells, which are then sucked out with a vacuum pump or syringe. Doctors warn that liposuction and other fat-busting procedures like tummy tucks do not in themselves solve the problem of obesity. Only a sensible diet and exercise can do this.

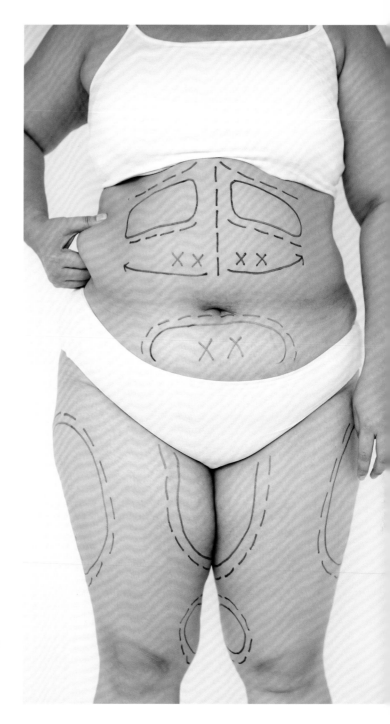

▲ Marks made by a cosmetic surgeon on an overweight patient's body indicate the range of fat-removal and body-reshaping operations available.

NON-SURGICAL TREATMENTS

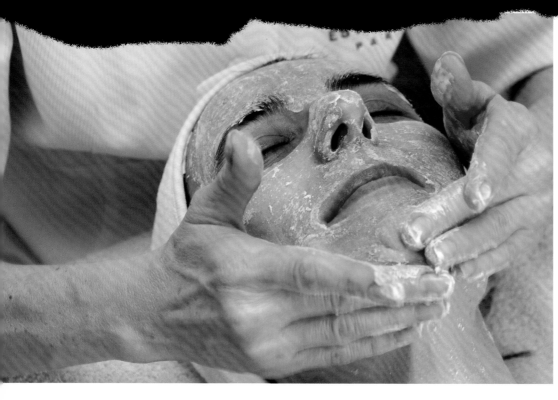

◄ There are various non-surgical treatments – such as this peel – available to combat facial wrinkles and help ageing skin.

NON-SURGICAL COSMETIC procedures include treatments like chemical injections to smooth out wrinkles and skin peels to make skin look healthier. These treatments appeal to many people because they are usually quicker and cheaper than surgery – but the people who carry out the treatments may not always have adequate training or skills.

THE BOTOX EFFECT

Botox is the best-known non-surgical cosmetic procedure – although few people know it is actually a diluted version of the food poison Botulinum toxin. Botox works by paralysing then relaxing the facial muscles used in frowning and raising the eyebrows, removing wrinkles and other skin lines. Its effects last three to four months, which means people may have Botox injections over and over again. Repeated use, however, can cause the muscles to thin, reducing the range of facial expressions.

SKIN DEEP

Other types of non-surgical cosmetic procedure include peels, which remove the top layer of skin to improve skin quality, treat wrinkles and spots, and even remove tattoos. Microdermabrasion is a peel procedure in which the therapist sprays tiny particles onto the skin, before vacuuming them off. Another treatment uses lasers to vaporize the surface layers of the skin. Spice Girl singer, Geri Halliwell, has paid for laser treatment to remove an unwanted tattoo from her back.

FILLERS

Just as some treatments involve sucking things out, so others involve putting things back in. Silicon, hyaluronic acid and collagen are "fillers" that cosmetic surgeons and beauty therapists use to fill out wrinkles and scars, as well as lips. Collagen is a liquid made from the connective tissue of pigs and cows. A small percentage of people have an allergic reaction to collagen, so everyone should be tested before having a collagen injection. Unfortunately this test is not completely accurate, so some people will still have a bad reaction to collagen.

▼ Laser tattoo removal is a popular non-surgical procedure.

GET THE FACTS STRAIGHT

The top five non-surgical cosmetic procedures in the USA in 2006 were:

- Botox injection (3,181,592 procedures),
- Hyaluronic acid (1,593,554 procedures),
- Laser hair removal (1,475,296 procedures),
- Microdermabrasion (993,071 procedures),
- Laser skin resurfacing (576,509 procedures).

(Source: The American Society for Aesthetic Plastic Surgery)

COSMETIC SURGERY and non-surgical treatments can be expensive, painful, time-consuming and even embarrassing to admit to. Why then do so many people go through with it? Time after time the answer is the same: to increase self-confidence.

LIFE-CHANGING

There is little doubt that cosmetic surgery can improve people's self-esteem and allow them to get on with their lives. Both cosmetic and plastic surgery can be particularly helpful for people living with disfigurements, as well as for people who are scarred after accidents or cancer treatment. Breast reduction operations can take away the back and neck pain that some women suffer, while children and teenagers who are teased because of unusual ears, for example, can benefit from surgery.

▼ Cosmetic surgery can have life-changing benefits. UK teenager Harriet Fulcher was seriously disfigured after being hit by a car in 2004. This photograph shows the extensive scars from the hours of surgery she had to undergo.

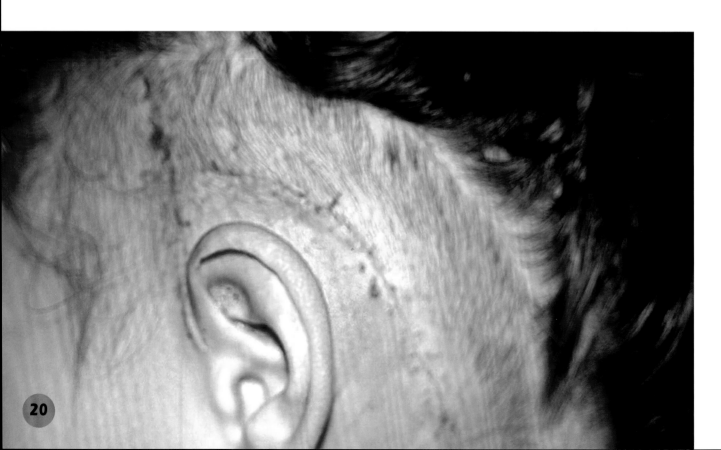

▲ Harriet Fulcher after her recovery. Thanks to a combination of neurosurgery and cosmetic surgery, her face was rebuilt and she can smile again.

BODY BOOSTS

People without such obvious problems can also receive an enormous confidence boost from cosmetic surgery. Put simply, looking good can help us feel good. Professor Lawrence Kirwan, who practises cosmetic surgery in the US and the UK, says it is this confidence that most of his patients are seeking: "The majority of my patients don't come to me and ask me to make them beautiful. They want to look the way they feel, or correct something that makes them feel unattractive and unhappy."

AGE CONCERN

Some of the benefits of cosmetic surgery are less comfortable to consider. Thanks to the power of advertising and the media, images of young and beautiful people can result in feelings of shame about the physical signs of ageing, from wrinkles to sagging skin. Face-lifts, Botox injections and a variety of nips and tucks can – for a while at least – hide these natural signs. But what does this say about our values and our attitude to older people?

NO SURGERY is risk-free:

operations can and do go wrong, resulting in scarring, infections and, occasionally, death. The difference with cosmetic surgery is that it is surgery someone has voluntarily chosen to have, often in order to look better. This can make it particularly hard for patients and their relatives when things go wrong.

FATAL SURGERY

One example of cosmetic surgery that ended tragically was the procedure carried out in 2005 on Stella Obasanjo, wife of the then Nigerian president, Olusegun Obasanjo. Mrs Obasanjo had travelled from Nigeria to Spain for what Nigerian newspapers said was a tummy tuck operation. Because of complications during surgery, however, Mrs Obasanjo was rushed to a local hospital Accident and Emergency department, but was dead on arrival.

▲ Stella Obasanjo, who died when a cosmetic surgery procedure went wrong in 2005.

RISK FACTORS

Complications during cosmetic surgery – like all surgery – can result in heart attack, blood clot or haemorrhage. The reality is that deaths from cosmetic surgery are fairly rare, but procedures can sometimes result in infections or permanent scarring. There are examples of nose jobs going wrong, causing the entire nose to collapse. Breast implants can burst inside the body, making it very difficult for a woman to breast-feed if she goes on to have a child.

FACING THE ISSUES

Here are some other high-profile examples of cosmetic surgery that has gone badly wrong:

- In 2002, a liposuction operation on Denise Hendry, wife of the former Scotland football captain Colin Hendry, left her with septicaemia (blood poisoning). She spent five weeks in a coma.

- In 2004, the American novelist Olivia Goldsmith had a fatal heart attack while under anaesthetic before she was due to have surgery on her chin.

- In 2007, Donda West, mother of American hip-hop star Kanye West, died the day after cosmetic surgery that included liposuction, breast reduction and a tummy tuck. It was thought West may not have been in a fit state to undergo this intensive surgery.

OBJECTIVE INFORMATION?

Public awareness of the risks associated with cosmetic surgery is limited. People who decide to have treatment often get their information from TV, the Internet or magazines, rather than discussing it with a family doctor. In 2007 the UK Advertising Standards Agency banned a poster campaign by the London-based Harley Medical Group because it failed to inform people of the risks involved in cosmetic surgery. The banned poster carried the message "Gorgeous breasts just got easy with cosmetic surgery".

▼ Even simple cosmetic procedures, such as Botox injections, carry risks.

SURGERY ADDICTS

FOR SOME PEOPLE, the quest for "perfection" through cosmetic surgery can be highly addictive. The consequences can be extreme – both physically and psychologically.

READ ALL ABOUT IT

In 2006 American writer and journalist, Alex Kuczynski, published her book *Beauty Junkies: Getting Under the Skin of the Cosmetic Surgery Industry*. In it she describes how people can become addicted to cosmetic surgery. Kuczynski writes from personal experience: over eight years she had regular Botox injections and microdermabrasion, as well as liposuction and eyelid and lip-plumping treatments.

BODY DYSMORPHIC DISORDER

Sometimes a psychological condition can drive someone to have repeated cosmetic surgery. This can be depression or extremely low self-esteem, or may be body dysmorphic disorder (BDD). People with BDD are obsessed with correcting some aspect of their appearance that no one else may be aware of, such as a tiny scar. Most

▲ Jocelyne Wildenstein, the "cat woman" (see right).

cosmetic surgeons refuse to operate on people with BDD, partly because to do so would be unethical; partly because there is a strong chance the sufferer will never be satisfied with the result.

STRANGER THAN FICTION

A well-known example of someone who has had multiple cosmetic surgery operations, with dramatic results, is Jocelyne Wildenstein, known in tabloid newspapers as "the cat woman". Wildenstein, who was born in Switzerland, has had numerous silicone and collagen injections, as well as face-lifts and eye reconstruction surgery, to give her face a cat-like appearance.

▶ Pop star Michael Jackson's appearance as a child in the 1970s (top) and by the 1990s (right). How much cosmetic surgery was involved?

FACING THE ISSUES

Probably the most talked-about person in the world when it comes to the subject of cosmetic surgery is the pop superstar Michael Jackson. Over the course of the 1980s, Jackson's skin became paler and paler, leading some black people in the USA and elsewhere to say that he was trying to look white. Jackson denied these accusations, and said his changing skin colour was the result of vitiligo, a disease which causes the loss of melanin pigment in the skin. Jackson has admitted to a few cosmetic surgery operations, to his nose and chin. Many journalists and even cosmetic surgeons, however, think he has had many more procedures, resulting in profound changes to his appearance.

TEENAGE SURGERY

MANY TEENAGERS want to have cosmetic surgery for much the same reasons as adults. In the USA in 2006, for example, 40,464 surgical procedures and 137,577 non-surgical procedures were performed on people aged 18 or younger. Unlike adults, however, teenagers' bodies are still growing, so cosmetic surgery might not always be a sensible choice.

BIRTHDAY WISH

In 2001, 15-year-old Jenna Franklin, from Nottinghamshire in the UK, made the headlines when journalists found out that her mother had agreed to her request for a breast enlargement operation for her 16th birthday. Jenna's mother, who owned her own cosmetic surgery business, told reporters, "I want Jenna to feel confident about the way she looks." Jenna added, "You've got to have breasts to be successful. Every other person you see on television has had implants."

GET THE FACTS STRAIGHT

Risks associated with breast implants include:

- Infection
- Haematoma (collection of blood caused by internal bleeding)
- Capsular contracture (painful hardening of the breasts)
- Loss of nipple sensation
- Scarring
- Interference with the lactation process (production of milk when breast-feeding)

◀ Media and advertising images of teenagers with perfect, tanned bodies can create feelings of inadequacy.

▲ In a world obsessed with superficial looks, is it any wonder that young people feel that surgery is desirable?

GROWING PAINS

Plenty of other teenagers would agree with Jenna. Magazine and Internet surveys around the world routinely report young people's dissatisfaction with their bodies. Boys feel pressure to look more muscular, while girls often worry about the size of their breasts, as well as their weight. The trouble is that teenagers' bodies are still developing, so not only might cosmetic surgery be physically dangerous (see box), but dissatisfactions you have with your body at the age of 15 might no longer exist by the time you are 18.

TIME TO REGULATE?

The Australian government is facing strong calls to regulate its cosmetic surgery industry in order to protect teenagers. There are no publicly available figures on the number of operations performed on teenagers in Australia, but there are reports of girls as young as 13 having operations to increase the size of their breasts. Among the Australian cosmetic surgeons backing the demand for regulation is Dr Cholm Williams of Sydney, who describes teenagers as "more vulnerable than society at large".

CHECKS AND BALANCES

WHO MONITORS the cosmetic surgery industry? What safeguards are there to protect people who should not have operations – because they are too young, have psychological problems or want surgery for the wrong reasons? The short answer is that, while there are some checks and balances in place, they probably do not go far enough. In the end, each of us has to take responsibility for the choices we make.

BACKGROUND CHECKS

While no one can call themselves a heart surgeon without training in both general and heart surgery, this does not apply to cosmetic surgeons. In countries such as Australia and the USA, for example, doctors without surgical training are legally allowed to perform cosmetic surgery. Professional bodies – such as the Australian Society of Plastic Surgeons and the American Society for Aesthetic Plastic Surgery – represent only cosmetic surgeons who have trained in both general surgery and facial and body procedures.

◄ Kanye West and his mother Donda, who paid the ultimate price for cosmetic surgery that she may not have been fit enough to undergo (see page 23).

QUESTION CHECKS

People who are considering cosmetic surgery bear some responsibility for ensuring that their cosmetic surgeon is registered with a professional body, that the surgeon is qualified to perform the particular procedure they want, and that they know about the risks involved in the surgery. Many of the same questions should be asked of those who offer non-surgical treatments, such as beauty therapists. For example, does the therapist belong to a professional body? Has he or she been trained to carry out the treatment?

PSYCHOLOGICAL CHECKS

Cosmetic surgeons who belong to professional associations are usually trained in screening procedures, also known as psychological tests. These enable a surgeon to tell if the patient is a suitable candidate for cosmetic surgery. Screening can reveal if a patient's expectations are too high, or if they are suffering from depression or BDD. It may also tell if someone is wanting surgery for a dubious reason, for example because their partner says they will find them more attractive.

▶ A cosmetic surgery professional discusses a nose procedure with a patient. Computer modelling can demonstrate what the results will look like.

GET THE FACTS STRAIGHT

In 2005, the UK government launched a website for people considering cosmetic surgery and non-surgical cosmetic treatments. The website contains questions people should ask themselves before embarking on cosmetic surgery, including:

- Do you expect it to change your life as well as your appearance, and how do you think your life will be better?

- Is it likely that a change in your appearance will radically change your life?

- Are you considering surgery for yourself, or to please someone else?

- Do you think having surgery will improve your relationship or your employment prospects?

(Source: www.dh.gov.uk/en/Publichealth/ CosmeticSurgery)

THE SURGEONS

WHAT DO WE KNOW about cosmetic surgeons themselves? What are their views on their industry, and the role of cosmetic surgery in society? Find out about some of the top cosmetic surgeons, from Brazil, the USA and the UK.

IVO PITANGUY

In Brazil, a country famous for its obsession with beautiful bodies, the cosmetic surgeon Ivo Pitanguy (right) is known as "the professor". He has performed more than 50,000 operations, many on the wealthiest people in Brazil as well as from abroad. But Pitanguy also runs a public plastic surgery clinic which provides free surgery for people who cannot afford the costs. "The better we look, the better we feel about ourselves, rich or poor," Pitanguy has said. "I am trying to make cosmetic surgery something that everyone has a right to."

FACING THE ISSUES

There can often be rivalry and even tension between plastic surgeons and cosmetic surgeons. Plastic surgeons have accused cosmetic surgeons of trivialising their work in treating cancer patients, burns victims and people born with disfigurements, such as cleft palates. In turn, cosmetic surgeons say that some of the techniques they have developed have benefited plastic surgery.

Cosmetic surgeons can earn more money than plastic surgeons – one reason for the rivalry between them. Peter Butler, a UK plastic surgeon who specialises in face transplants, said if he were to become a cosmetic surgeon he could increase his salary by ten times.

SHERRELL ASTON

Dr Sherrell Aston is one of the top cosmetic surgeons in the USA. He is the director of the Department of Plastic Surgery at the Manhattan Eye, Ear and Throat Hospital, in New York, which carries out more cosmetic surgery operations each year than anywhere else in the world. Aston is rumoured to have performed surgery on celebrities including the French actress Catherine Deneuve and former US senator Bob Dole. In 2007, Aston's hospital paid $3.1 million to the husband of a woman who died after reacting badly to painkillers before having cosmetic surgery.

▲ Dr Sherrell Aston (far left) pictured with, from left, his wife, Robert Di Niro and Grace Hightower.

ADAM SEARLE

Adam Searle is a British cosmetic surgeon and, like Aston, a past president of his country's professional association (in Searle's case, the British Association of Aesthetic Plastic Surgeons). Searle is thoughtful about the place of cosmetic surgery in society: "It can alter the lives of those who need it," he says. "But I fear we may be stepping into a gratuitous cosmetic surgery trap, where people tumble into having multiple procedures as if it's a hairdo. Yet it carries very real risks, which have to be taken into account."

◄ Adam Searle is one of the UK's top cosmetic surgeons

VIEWING FIGURES

STORIES ABOUT COSMETIC SURGERY help sell
newspapers and magazines, and "extreme" makeover programmes – in
which participants undergo cosmetic surgery – regularly attract large
audiences. Many of us are fascinated with cosmetic surgery, but is media
coverage increasing this fascination or simply reflecting it?

HORSES FOR COURSES

Different media tend to focus on different
aspects of cosmetic surgery. Newspapers
and Internet news sites generally
concentrate on horror stories in which
cosmetic surgery has gone badly wrong,
following the well-worn cliché that bad
news sells. Magazines, and in particular
women's and teenage girls' magazines

(above), are more interested in the range of
cosmetic surgery procedures available and
whether they are effective or not. TV dramas
look at more emotional issues. The US-made
"Nip/Tuck" follows the lives of two cosmetic
surgeons based in Los Angeles. "Tell me
what you don't like about yourself" is the
show's catch-phrase.

EXTREME MAKEOVERS

For TV producers, the main focus on cosmetic surgery is the extreme makeover programme, a format which – like "Big Brother" – has spread all over the world. Examples in the UK include "10 Years Younger" and "Cosmetic Surgery Live", and in the USA "The Swan" and "I Want A Famous Face". In 2007 a show in Spain, "Cambio Radical", ran into controversy for offering free cosmetic surgery to those willing to take part in the programme.

RAISING CONCERNS

Some people – including politicians, cosmetic surgeons and health experts – are concerned that cosmetic surgery makeover shows do not fully explain the risks involved in surgery, and can make the process appear easy. There are also concerns that these programmes can raise people's expectations about what cosmetic surgery can achieve for them, whether it be radically altering the way they look or dramatically improving their lives.

◄ From "frumpy" to "glamorous" – these two photos show the before and after of an extreme makeover. TV shows featuring these kind of changes are very popular with the viewing public.

WHAT DO YOU THINK?

● Are you interested in watching or reading about cosmetic surgery?

● Why do you think the media is interested in cosmetic surgery?

● Do you think the media influences people to have cosmetic surgery – or do you think it just reflects people's interests?

● Some people think cosmetic surgery makeover programmes are an invasion of people's privacy. Do you agree?

FEMINIST thinkers – who believe that women should be equal to men in every aspect of their lives – are divided when it comes to the question of cosmetic surgery. Some see it as empowering for women; others regard it as another example of pressure from a male-dominated system designed to control women.

▲ US writer Naomi Wolf, who believes that cosmetic surgery maintains women's insecurities and lack of control.

WOMEN vs MEN

Around nine out of every ten cosmetic surgery patients are women. Does this statistic tell us something about women's and men's different attitudes to their bodies? The British feminist writer Catherine Redfern argues that there are two major assumptions that Western societies make about women's bodies: firstly that "something is fundamentally wrong with the female body and it's natural to be unhappy about it", and secondly that "if we're unhappy about our bodies we should change them".

THE POLITICS OF BEAUTY

This view is similar to the one put forward by the American writer Naomi Wolf in *The Beauty Myth*. Wolf argues that ideas about beauty have been controlled by men to keep women under their power. Wolf describes how images of "ideal" women's bodies in the media, and the promise of transformation through cosmetic surgery, prey on women's insecurities. In her own words: "We are in the midst of a violent backlash against feminism that uses images of female beauty as a political weapon against women's advancement."

WINNING SMILES

The American psychologist and writer, Nancy Etcoff, disputes Wolf's argument, saying instead that beauty is not a myth but a universal measure of how attractive someone is. Other women – and men – agree, pointing out that better-looking people of both sexes are more likely to be successful in work and possibly in relationships. People on Etcoff's side of the debate see cosmetic surgery as a way of improving on what nature has given us.

WHAT DO YOU THINK?

- Do you think women tend to have more negative attitudes to their bodies than men? If so, why do you think this is?

- Do you think there is any truth in the argument that beauty is a "myth" controlled by men?

- Do you think beauty is subjective ("in the eye of the beholder") or objective (a universal standard)?

- Do you agree that better-looking people are more likely to be successful?

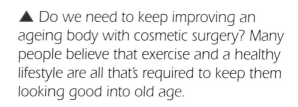

▲ Do we need to keep improving an ageing body with cosmetic surgery? Many people believe that exercise and a healthy lifestyle are all that's required to keep them looking good into old age.

BOOM AND BUST

WITH NEARLY 11.5 MILLION surgical and non-surgical procedures carried out in the USA alone in 2006, cosmetic surgery is big business. And like all big businesses, some people are making a lot of money while others are spending a lot.

▼ Countries with a strong beach culture, such as Brazil and Spain, have high levels of cosmetic surgery procedures.

BIG FIGURES

Just how much is the cosmetic surgery industry worth around the world? In 2005, Americans spent approximately $12.4 billion on cosmetic surgery – more than the value of all the goods and services produced in some developing countries. Brazil and Spain are, respectively, second and third in the world, both in terms of spending on cosmetic surgery and the number of procedures carried out.

FACING THE ISSUES

Cosmetic surgery tourism is part of the wider phenomenon of medical tourism, which has grown into a worldwide, multibillion dollar industry. The biggest attraction for many medical tourists is cost – the top destinations, such as India, Cuba, Lithuania and Thailand, offer treatment at much lower prices than in countries such as the USA or in Europe.

There are other reasons why people head abroad for operations and treatment, including frustration with hospital waiting lists back home. But problems associated with medical tourism include the often non-existent follow-up care for patients who return home after treatment, and criticism that such tourists divert medical resources away from local communities.

HOLIDAYS WITH A TWIST

One way that cosmetic surgery clinics boost their takings is by attracting so-called surgery tourists from abroad. Brazil is one of the top destinations for such tourists, who typically come for surgery and a relaxing holiday afterwards – a chance to allow stitches to heal before going home. Argentina is another favourite surgery tourism destination; others include South Africa and Mexico.

I.O.U.

Surgery costs a lot of money. In the UK, for example, the price of operations ranges from about £3,500 to £12,000. There is little chance that governments or private medical insurers will pay for this treatment, so people who want surgery often have no choice but to take out a loan. Banks in the UK estimated that in 2008 they would loan as much as £1.4 billion to people who wanted cosmetic surgery. It is worth noting that the UK has the highest level of personal debt in Europe.

► Plastic surgery? With cosmetic surgery not covered by many insurers, many people who cannot afford procedures will be tempted to pay with credit.

DO YOU LIKE the way you look? Maybe you think your nose is a bit large, or you wish you were slimmer, curvier, more muscular. You are not alone! But having cosmetic surgery may not be the best way to become happy with yourself.

▲ The best way to control weight is through diet and exercise, not surgery.

SENSIBLE STEPS

Health experts, and many cosmetic surgeons, recognise that cosmetic surgery is not the way to deal with weight problems. Procedures like liposuction and tummy tucks may be acceptable as a way of reshaping fatty deposits that do not respond to diet and exercise, but they do not stop future weight gain. The only sensible way to reduce weight is to watch what you eat, to eat sensibly and to take regular exercise.

GETTING DEEP

Looking after yourself in terms of eating well and exercising can also help you feel good about yourself. Seeking ways to improve self-confidence is an alternative to cosmetic surgery. Our attitude towards ourselves makes a big difference to how attractive other people find us. No one is saying that looks are unimportant, but deep down it is who we are, not how we look, that determines our happiness.

EXTRA HELP

Of course, eating sensibly, taking exercise and improving self-confidence are often easier said than done. Sometimes we need more help. Friends and family members can offer support; at other times it can be helpful to discuss concerns about the way we look or think about ourselves with a counsellor or therapist. These professionals can offer support and help people understand why they feel and behave the way they do, as well as the choices available to them.

▼ Discussing issues with a counsellor can be helpful for a person's self-esteem.

GET THE FACTS STRAIGHT

- Don't smoke, or drink excessively: it ruins your skin and your health.

- Eat fresh fruit and vegetables, complex carbohydrates (like brown bread, rice and pasta), foods rich in Omega-3 fatty acids (like oily fish) and drink lots of water.

- Dress clever: choose clothes to flatter your figure. Remember that vertical stripes are slimming and a padded bra is a lot less hassle than breast implants!

- Pamper yourself: a new haircut, new grooming products and new or second-hand clothes can work wonders for your self-confidence.

WILL COSMETIC surgery become even more popular in the years ahead? What new techniques will cosmetic surgeons develop to boost our bodies and flatter our features? Perhaps the biggest question, however, is how much influence cosmetic surgery will continue to have on the way we see ourselves.

SOCIAL DIVIDE

An argument made in the USA and elsewhere is that cosmetic surgery creates a further division between rich and poor – in this case, between those who can afford to pay for surgery and treatments and those who cannot. The risk, according to this viewpoint, is that people with low incomes will increasingly stand out and be stigmatised as the one group who cannot correct their bad teeth or prematurely ageing faces.

A BEAUTY STANDARD?

Another argument is that, thanks to the global advertising and entertainment industries, a predominantly Western and white "beauty standard" is fast becoming established around the world. Cosmetic surgery is playing its part in this standard, the argument goes, enabling models and actors from non-Western countries to change their looks.

▲ British-born actor Orlando Bloom, considered by many to set a standard for film-star male attractiveness. Will even more widely available cosmetic surgery mean that actors from non-Western countries will strive to alter their appearance?

▲ This photograph of a crowd demonstrates the diversity of human faces. Wouldn't it be tragic if, at some point in the future, this diversity were to be modified in favour of one standard of "beauty"?

SAME OLD STORY

New trends often turn out to have old roots, however. A recent development in cosmetic surgery is for operations to shorten toes or narrow feet, to allow women to wear designer high-heeled shoes, for example. But this has strong parallels with the practice of foot binding, common in China from the 10th to the 20th centuries. The practice, in which young girls' feet were wrapped in tight bandages to prevent normal growth – resulting in painful bone damage – was in order to fit an ideal standard of beauty.

GET THE FACTS STRAIGHT

New cosmetic surgery procedures appear all the time. Here are three recent ones:

● Liposelection: this procedure is similar to liposuction, but involves the use of ultrasound (high-frequency sound waves) to liquefy fat before removing it.

● Internal bra: the surgeon places a surgical dressing under the skin to lift the breast. The dressing acts exactly as if the patient is wearing a permanent bra.

● Threadlift: a quicker version of a face-lift. The surgeon makes a small incision in the brow, implants threads with tiny "teeth" and then pulls them up to tighten loose skin.

GLOSSARY

anaesthetic: A drug or gas which produces a loss of feeling and pain. General anaesthetics work on the whole body while local anaesthetics work on a part of the body.

beauty therapist: Someone who works in a beauty clinic and carries out beauty treatments, which may include non-surgical cosmetic procedures. Beauty therapists should ideally be trained to carry out such procedures.

chin job: Cosmetic surgery to make a person's chin look larger (mentoplasty) or smaller (genioplasty). Making a chin look larger involves the use of a chin implant, which may be made of silicone, other artificial materials or body tissue.

cleft palate: A condition some people have at birth, caused by the plates in the roof of the mouth failing to close. This can be associated with a cleft lip – a fissure or crack in the lip beneath the nose. Children with a cleft palate have problems sucking and, later, speaking. Surgery can successfully overcome both cleft palates and cleft lips.

coma: A state of deep unconsciousness, usually caused by injury to the brain.

cosmetic surgery: An operation or operations, chosen by the patient, to modify an aspect of their appearance.

counsellor: Someone who offers a professional listening or support service to help an individual work through their problems.

disfigurement: Damage or scarring to someone's face, either as a result of a birth defect, an accident or illness.

feminism: A belief that men and women should be equal in social, political and economic terms.

First World War: A major conflict between 1914 and 1918 involving the Allies (including France, Great Britain, Italy, Japan, Australia and, from 1917, the USA) against the Central Powers (Germany, the Ottoman Empire and Austro-Hungary).

haemorrhage: Heavy bleeding caused by damaged blood vessels.

melanin: Black or dark brown pigment (a colour-producing substance) in the hair, skin and eyes.

nose job: An operation to reshape the nose or relieve blockages in the nostrils.

plastic surgery: Surgery to reconstruct facial and bodily disfigurements that result from birth problems, accidents or illnesses.

psychological: Something that occurs in the mind rather than the body. One common psychological condition is depression.

regulation: Laws or rules that control how something works. Regulations for cosmetic surgery could include banning surgery for under-18s.

rehabilitation: The process of restoring someone to health and/or the ability to take part in society.

Second World War: A war that involved most countries of the world between 1939 and 1945, on either the side of the Axis Powers (Germany, Japan and Italy) or the Allies (France, Great Britain, the United States and the Soviet Union).

self-esteem: Having respect for, and thinking positively about, yourself.

skin graft: A procedure which involves taking skin from one part of a person's body to another part (e.g. from the arm to the nose) or from one person to a different person.

solarium: A special room or bed that uses ultraviolet light to enable the body to tan quickly.

Websites

The American Society for Aesthetic Plastic Surgery
http://www.surgery.org

The Australian Society of Plastic Surgeons
http://www.plasticsurgery.org.au

Changing Faces
Website of a UK-based charity that supports and represents people with disfigurements.
www.changingfaces.org.uk

Extreme Cosmetics
Informative site about cosmetic surgery.
http://www.bbc.co.uk/science/hottopics/extremecosmetics/index.shtml

Plastic Surgery Addiction
Part of Ohio State University's Body Image and Health Task Force.
http://hec.osu.edu/bitf/PlasticSurgery.htm

Project Façade
A website based on an exhibition about the use and development of plastic surgery and prostheses (artificial body parts) in the First World War.
http://www.projectfacade.com

Teenage Plastic Surgery
A good site for young people with lots of information about plastic and cosmetic surgery.
http://www.kidshealth.org/teen/your_mind/body_image/plastic_surgery.html

10 Years Younger
Website about this UK cosmetic surgery makeover programme.
http://www.channel4.com/life/microsites/0-9/10yy/index.html

The British Association of Aesthetic Plastic Surgeons
http://www.baaps.org.uk

Every effort has been made by the Publishers to ensure that the websites in this book are suitable for children, that they are of the highest educational value, and that they contain no inappropriate or offensive material. However, because of the nature of the Internet, it is impossible to guarantee that the contents of these sites will not be altered. We strongly advise that Internet access is supervised by a responsible adult.

INDEX

accidents 9, 20, 42
addicts, surgery 24-25
Aston, Dr Sherrell 31

beauty, ideals of 10, 34, 35, 40, 41
Bloom, Orlando 40
botox see injections, botox
breasts,
    implants 8, 16, 17, 23, 26, 27, 39
    reductions 16, 17, 20, 23

collagen 19, 25

diet 17, 38-39
disfigurements 9, 13, 14, 20, 30, 42, 43
disorder, body dysmorphic (BDD)
    24, 29

Elizabeth I 10
Etcoff, Nancy 35
exercise 17, 35, 38-39

face-lifts 8, 14, 16, 21, 25, 41
fillers 19
First World War 11, 12-13, 42, 43

Gillies, Sir Harold 13
grafts, skin 11, 13, 43

Hiroshima 13
Hollywood 14

illnesses 9, 20
injections, botox 8, 15, 18, 19, 21,
    23, 24

Jackson, Michael 25

Kirwan, Lawrence 21
Kuczynski, Alex 24

liposuction 16, 17, 23, 24, 38, 41

McIndoe, Archibald 13
media, role of 8, 21, 32-33, 34, 40
microdermabrasion 19, 24
Monroe, Marilyn 14

nose, operations on 10, 11, 14, 16, 23,
    25, 29, 42, 43

Obasanjo, Stella 22

Padaung 11
peels, skin 18, 19
Pitanguy, Ivo 30

Redfern, Catherine, 34
regulation 27, 28-29, 42

Searle, Adam 31
scarring 9, 10, 20, 22, 23, 27, 42
Second World War 12-13, 14, 43

self-confidence 9, 20-21, 30, 39
shows, TV makeover 8, 32, 33, 43
solariums 21, 43
surgery, cosmetic
    benefits of 9, 20-21
    cost of 36, 37
    risks 9, 22-23, 27, 28, 29, 31, 33

teenagers 20, 26-27, 37, 43
The Beauty Myth 34-35
tourism, medical 37
treatments,
    non-surgical 8, 18-19
    surgical 8, 16-17, 41
tuck, tummy 8, 16, 17, 22, 23, 38

West, Donda 9, 23, 28
Wildenstein, Jocelyne 24, 25
Wolf, Naomi 34, 35

Here are the lists of contents for each title in *Science in the News*:

CLIMATE CHANGE

WHAT IS CLIMATE CHANGE? • CLIMATE CHANGE SCIENCE • CLIMATE SCIENCE HISTORY
CLIMATE CHANGE IN THE PAST • CAUSES OF CLIMATE CHANGE • CARBON DIOXIDE EMISSIONS
THE EFFECTS OF CLIMATE CHANGE • CLIMATE CHANGE REPORTS • PIONEER PRESSURE GROUPS
CLIMATE-CHANGE SUMMITS • GOVERNMENT REACTIONS • NEW INDUSTRIAL NATIONS
CONTINUING PROTESTS • AGAINST THE FLOW • CARBON REDUCTION • PREDICTING THE FUTURE
RESPONDING TO CLIMATE CHANGE

ORGAN TRANSPLANTATION

INTRODUCTION • IN THE BEGINNING • WORLD FIRSTS • ORGAN CRISIS • PRESUMED CONSENT
LIFE FROM LIFE • RELIGION & CULTURE • ARTIFICIAL ORGANS • XENOTRANSPLANTATION
STEM CELL RESEARCH • THE RIGHT TO AN ORGAN? • TRANSPLANT TOURISTS • ORGAN SELLERS
REGULATING THE TRADE • POST-OPERATIVE LIFE • FACE TRANSPLANTS • NEW BREAKTHROUGHS

COSMETIC SURGERY

INTRODUCTION • ANCIENT ORIGINS • THE FIRST AND SECOND WORLD WARS
FROM HOLLYWOOD TO THE HIGH STREET • SURGICAL TREATMENTS • NON-SURGICAL TREATMENTS
THE BENEFITS • THE RISKS • SURGERY ADDICTS • TEENAGE SURGERY • CHECKS AND BALANCES
THE SURGEONS • VIEWING FIGURES • "THE BEAUTY MYTH" • BOOM AND BUST
ALTERNATIVES • FACING THE FUTURE

NUCLEAR POWER

WHAT IS NUCLEAR POWER? • THE HISTORY OF NUCLEAR POWER
WHO USES NUCLEAR POWER? • NUCLEAR FUELS • NUCLEAR POWER STATIONS • NUCLEAR REACTOR TYPES
NUCLEAR POWER FOR TRANSPORT • NUCLEAR WASTE • BUILDING AND DECOMMISSIONING
NUCLEAR SAFETY • THE CHERNOBYL DISASTER • TERROR THREATS • ROGUE STATES
ANTI-NUCLEAR CAMPAIGNS • NUCLEAR POWER PLANS
NUCLEAR FUSION • THE NUCLEAR FUTURE

GENETICS

GENETIC MODIFICATION • DARWIN - FROM MONKEY TO MAN • IN THE GENES
A MASTER-RACE - A BREED APART? • ANIMAL ODDITIES • DNA - A CODE FOR LIVING
THE CHANGING CODE • RECESSIVE GENES - A HIDDEN INHERITANCE • ARE GM CROPS FRANKENSTEIN FOODS?
DANGEROUS MEDDLING? • MAKING MONSTERS? • "GENETIC FINGERPRINTS" • TRACING YOUR ROOTS • NATURE AND NUTURE
ALTERED INHERITANCE • CLONING - A CARBON COPY? • A LEGACY OR TIMEBOMB?

MAKING A NEW LIFE

CREATING LIFE • THE MAGIC OF LIFE • MOTHERS AND SONS • ARTIFICIAL INSEMINATION
PARENTAL RESPONSIBILITY • IVF - THE TEST TUBE BABY • MULTIPLE PREGNANCIES • THE GIFT OF LIFE
SURROGACY - TWO MOTHERS? • TOO OLD FOR PARENTHOOD? • CHECKING PROGRESS
SONS OR DAUGHTERS? • SAVIOUR SIBLINGS • FROZEN FOR THE FUTURE • WHAT IS A CLONE?
HUMAN CLONES • CREATING LIFE IN THE FUTURE